in a
HURRY

Ancient
Greece

written and drawn by
JOHN FARMAN

First published 1998 by Macmillan Children's Books
a division of Macmillan Publishers Limited
25 Eccleston Place, London SW1W 9NF
and Basingstoke

Associated companies throughout the world

ISBN 0 330 35249 0

3 5 7 9 8 6 4

A CIP catalogue record for this book is available from
the British Library.

Printed and bound in Great Britain
by Mackays of Chatham plc, Kent

✑ CONTENTS

OFF WE GO!

I've been to Greece a couple of times and jolly nice it was too. Sunny, friendly, quiet, the odd geriatric donkey being led slowly down a dusty street by a sun-shrunken old man, a whiskery old crone, bent double in widow's black, carrying a fat round loaf home from the village bakery . . . Greece redefines the word 'slow'. Nothing ever seems to happen there and nobody notices if it does. In fact, it's so laid back that just talking about it is enough to send you into a long, deep sleeeeeeeeeeeeeeeeeeee . . .*

Sorry . . . How amazing, therefore, to even consider that from 800 to 300 BC the Greeks led the world in just about everything from science to music to art to architecture to writing to philosophy to mathematics to . . . well, everything. It was a mighty ancient civilization whose influence in all things is still with us today. How is it that such a fantastically go-ahead place, having reached such dizzy heights, could then disappear almost without trace? I'll tell you.

PS You'll probably notice grumpy little comments (like the one below) throughout the book. Sorry, but that's my editor, Susie; she hasn't got much of a life, poor dear.

Chapter 1

GREECE GROWS UP
(THE HISTORICAL BIT)

Greece today is quite a big little country: around 50,000 square miles (Britain's 94,000). It lies gently sunbathing by the northeastern edge of the Mediterranean sea and has loads of islands (over a hundred) dotted around and about. If you'd like to know what they're called, my editor's simply dying to name them all for you.*

Greece used to be quite a bit smaller than it is today, but during World War I they nicked quite a bit of Turkey (leg or

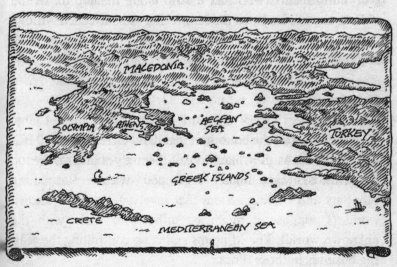

*Oh no I'm not. Ed

breast?), which is probably why the two countries still aren't speaking (actually, they hate each other's guts).

Hello Hellas

The very old name for Ancient Greece was Hellas and the people that lived there called themselves, quite understandably, the Hellenes (which means . . . Greeks). Quite sensible really. If that isn't good enough for you, these Hellenes probably came from one of the Pelasgian tribes who'd been settled in those parts for 40,000 years. The Hellenes were themselves divided into four tribes:

- The Aeolians (north).
- The Dorians (gathered round Mount Oeta).
- The Achaeans (who occupied the biggest bit of the southern part – called the Peloponnese).
- The Ionians (who had a strip along the top bit of the Peloponnese and also the area round Athens called Attica).

Crikey, this is boring. I'll move on.

Creating Crete

The first proper Greek civilization came about on the large island of Crete off the bottom of mainland Greece by 2000 BC. The Minoans, as they liked to call themselves (after their top god Minos), were highly organized, with a flourishing economy and trading system that involved all of the known world (I suppose it might be difficult to trade with the unknown world). The Minoans ended up controlling the seas. Big business in those times.

Useless Legend No. 529

There was this god called Zeus, who fell in love with a gorgeous princess called Europa. For some reason best known to himself, he turned into a bull and swam to Crete with the girl riding him (I suppose a bird on the back is worth two in . . .*). Anyway, one of their sons was called Minos and became king of Crete (actually all their kings were called Minos).

Plush Palaces

The Minoans built themselves massive palaces, sometimes up to four storeys in height, with huge apartments for their kings and queens. Their style of living was quite advanced (running water and colour tellies in every room). They had wonderfully detailed and beautifully painted frescoes on their walls and it's from digging these up that we've been able to learn so much about how they lived.

*Enough! Ed

Dead Nice

It's obvious from these frescoes that the Minoans were a very religious people, and it's quite nice to note, for a change, that they seemed to prefer their goddesses to their gods. Like many primitive people, they believed in an afterlife and would therefore provide their deceased rellies with food, drink and most of their lifetime possessions when they buried them, so they'd be dead comfortable when dead.

Useless Fact No. 532

Women of all classes dressed in a most unusual way. They wore these quite ordinary, down-to-the-ground frocks (with frilly layers, like Spanish dancers) but would have their boobs totally exposed. Funny that.

Bang!

Then suddenly it was all gone. In 1450 BC all the palaces disappeared due to volcanic eruptions (very popular down that way), and there might well have been the odd tidal wave and mass crop destruction.

If that wasn't bad enough, the king of the time (you're right – Minos) was murdered by a local other king who also trashed the precious Minoan fleet.

To cap it all, they were invaded and conquered by the Mycenaeans. It really wasn't their year. It seems that from then on, however, the Mycenaeans simply squabbled amongst themselves and let all that the Minoans had achieved run down like a clockwork toy.

The whole Minoan business was over by 1200 BC.

Useless Legend No. 534

Once upon a time, an Athenian prince called Theseus went on his holidays to Crete where he met, fought and slew this weird half-bull half-man (and half-wit?) character called the Minotaur. Mr Minotaur lived in a labyrinth (like the London Underground without signs or trains*). When he went in to find the old bull/person, his girlfriend, Ariadne, gave him a reel of cotton so's he'd find his way back (no mobiles those days).

It all worked fine: Theseus killed the Minotaur, found his way back to Ariadne and they lived happily ever after. The End.

Tell you what, this is going a bit slowly so we'll make a time chart.

1600–1200 BC

The first proper Greek civilizations were ruled over by the Mycenaeans.

1194–1184 BC

THE TROJAN WAR

According to legend, this battle was all about a princess called Helen. All the local kings fancied her but she eventually married the Spartan King Menelaus, King Agamemnon of Mycene's brother. To cut a long story short, the naughty girl ran off with Paris (not *to* Paris). Helen and the young prince went straight to Troy (cos Paris's old man was the King of Troy), in what we now call Turkey. This, understandably, upset King Agamemnon (and no doubt Menelaus) so he laid siege to Troy and the Trojans for ten years – TEN YEARS! – before

* The London Underground doesn't have many signs or trains either. Ed

doing the old wooden horse stunt. Actually, there was a bit more to it than that.

Troy, you see, stood at the entrance to the Black Sea and it was through this little space that all Greece's corn had to travel. The Trojans had been severely interfering with the Greeks' food supplies, so they had to do something about it anyway.

1100–800 BC

This was the period known as the DARK AGES (nothing to do with *our* Dark Ages) and was certainly apt as far as Greece was concerned. The only result of a long period of darkness was a substantial rise in population. How odd!

c. 1000 BC

A people called the Dorians eased into Laconia in southern Greece, kicking out the poor inhabitants and setting up their own state called Sparta, which became the largest in Greece. They flourished until 630 BC when the fierce folk of a savage neighbouring state called Messenia suddenly decided they'd had enough and revolted against Spartan rule. They'd been conquered about 100 years before, you see. They stayed revolting for nigh on 17 years, by which time every young Spartan male had to become a soldier and endure the most horrid of conditions to make him tough – which is where the term 'spartan' comes from. They soon became by far the strongest military power in Greece. Unfortunately, however, when you have everyone playing at soldiers, other stuff like art, literature and science tends to take a bit of a back seat.

800–500 BC

This was the ARCHAIC PERIOD, a time when everything started buzzing again. The Greeks relearned how to write, which helped their greatest poet Homer in one way but, in another way, didn't – on account of his being blind. It was a

WHERE DID I PUT THAT BLASTED PEN

time of mass emigration and setting up colonies in Sicily, southern France and western Turkey because (a) there were becoming far too many of them, and (b) they kept arguing amongst themselves and having mini-wars.

600–500 BC

It was around this time that the Persians (who lived in what we now call Iran) started giving the Greeks a hard time. It was all because a Greek tribe called the Ionians, who the Persians had conquered ages ago, wouldn't lie down and take their medicine and kept complaining. The Persians decided to take it out on *all* the Greeks. At first the Athenians kept them at bay, but the perishing Persians came back under Xerxes in 480 BC and trashed them good and proper. After beating the Athenian army at Thermoplae they marched into Athens and burned it to the ground, probably because all the army had gone off to fight them somewhere else at sea. But Sparta began to realize that they were running a little short on soldiers, so over the next few years made a whole lot of sneaky pacts and alliances with all her neighbours in the Peloponnese (the southern part of Greece).

500–323 BC
THE CLASSICAL OR GOLDEN AGE

479 BC

The Greeks got together to form a humungous army led by Spartan boss Pausanias and completely wiped out the Persians at Plataea while their navy burned the Persian fleet which was parked up at Mykale. The Persians had, therefore, blown their chance of a complete takeover of mainland Greece. The Greeks' battles with the Persians went on for years, but despite all this it was the beginning of what is now called the Golden or Classical Age.

431 BC

All good things come to an end. The Spartans had become a trifle miffed at the meteoric success of the Athenians and the Peloponnesian War broke out.

430 BC

Both sides were knackered through continuous war and Athens suffered a rather undesirable plague which took out one in three of the population and depleted both sides so much that they decided to make friends.

415 BC

But they simply couldn't get on and eventually the Athenian army was wiped out by the Spartans at Syracuse in Scicily.

405 BC

Those pesky Persians gave the splendid Spartans loads of loot to build up their fleet. This they did, and captured 170 beached Athenian ships (their whole navy had gone ashore for a swift kebab at Aegospotami) and executed 4000 sailors. It was the last straw for the poor old Athenians.

404 BC
The war had literally torn the whole place apart and by now Athens was as good as finished – never to be the same again.

403 BC
Athens got back to some sort of democracy but didn't notice that, over its shoulder, to the north-east, Macedonia was becoming very powerful and pulling horrid faces at them. The Macedonians thought of themselves as Greek but the rest of the Greeks would have none of it, viewing them as oiks, probably because they couldn't understand a word they said. What those rest of the Greeks also didn't realize was that the

SPOT THE MACEDONIAN

Macedonians had a fab new king called Philip (Greeks called Philip? – ah yes!*) who was going from strength to strength, winning little wars left, right and centre, snatching more and more territory as he went.

337 BC
Bad news alert! Philip was assassinated. But good news, he left a son called Alexander from his wife Olympia, who he'd just dumped. Historical detectives are still trying to work out whether the wife or son had anything to do with the assassination.

336 BC
Philip's boy became king at twenty and went out on the 35,000-strong Alexander's All-Conquering World Tour determined to start with the Persians (which he did). He was to end up with the biggest empire in the ancient world and for that he became known as Alexander the Great. Everywhere he went he left Greeks to administer the various cities which, as you might imagine, eventually spread the Greek language and culture right across Asia Minor, Egypt, Afghanistan, India, Iran (and Charlotte Street in London). Oddly enough, Alexander rather got to like the Persians and started wearing their clothes and even married one of their girls called Roxane (see Unlikely Names for Emperors' Wives). Alexander died of a nasty cold in 323 BC.

323 BC
Start of the HELLENISTIC PERIOD (the age of Greek literature), which lasted until 30 BC. It all began when news came

*I suppose you are referring to our dear queen's husband? Ed

through of Alexander's death, and loads of Greek cities rebelled as they'd had quite enough of the cocky Macedonians. These rebellions turned into the Lamian Wars and were only really notable because the Greeks (well, the ones that weren't Macedonians) lost all of 'em. Alexander's baby (his missus was pregnant when he dropped off his perch) took over the

empire but had to be helped by his half-brother Philip Arrideus. But Alexander's old generals had other ideas and soon carved up the empire (and Alexander's mum and brother) for themselves. But they couldn't even agree on who was going to have what . . . and there were lots more wars for another fifty odd years.

281 BC
Three kingdoms eventually surfaced – the Kingdom of Ptolemy (which was over Egypt way), the Kingdom of

Seleucus (which took up most of Persia) and the Kingdom of Antigonas (which ruled Greece and Macedonia – well, Macedonia by then ruled Greece anyway). Luckily, Athens managed to wheedle a position as a neutral state and carried on as a centre for all things cultural and aesthetic (just like my home).*

All seemed to be running rather smoothly until reports came in that the southern colonies of Greece were being given a bit of a runaround by raiding Romans from Italy who were looking to expand their field of operations. Things got so bad that Philip V of Macedonia stepped in to help Hannibal (the well-known Carthaginian general – and elephant man) in his struggle against the Romans. Then the Antigonids (from Macedonia) pitched in and lost to the rapidly-growing-stronger Roman legions in 146 BC. This effectively meant that the whole of Greece suddenly became just another Roman province. The Greek Empire was no more. That's life, I suppose.

Chapter 2

☁= *HOW GREECE WAS RUN*

As we saw in the history bit, the Greek civilization ran from the beginnings of the Minoans to when those rough Romans came and took all their toys away. Things changed a lot over those nearly 2000 years, so, for the purposes of this extremely skinny book, I'll just dive in at the Golden Age which ran from about 500 BC to 323 BC.

Up until that time Greece had been divvied up into a whole lot of little city states – basically large towns with all the land surrounding them. These operated completely independently of each other, with their own armies, leaders, laws and goats. Some were huge, like Athens, and others small with only a few thousand people.

In the beginning each one had its own king (Greek kings were two-a-penny), but gradually they were taken over by any old rich, strong men who just walked in and seized power. This could not be allowed to continue, so in 500 BC, or thereabouts, a new system had to be found. This was called *democracy* (or 'rule by the people'), from the word *demos* (people) and *kratos* (strength, power).*

Democracy in Athens

Democracy these days means that everyone except people under 18 (shame!) has some say in how things are run through his or her vote (well, that's the theory, anyway), but in

*Show-off. Ed

Athens only proper citizens had these rights. That excluded women (how do you like that, girls?), foreigners and, of course, slaves. Athens and its surrounding area (Attica) were divided into lots of small communities called *demes* which were then grouped into 30 *trittyes* (10 for Athens, 10 for the country all around and 10 for the coastal bit). These *trittyes* were then grouped into 10 *phyles* (each made of 3 *trittyes* from city, country and coast). I hope you're remembering all this.

The Assembly

The Assembly, or *Pnyx,* came round once a month and every citizen had the right to vote on the issues of the day (laws, policies, parking, etc.) put to them by the Council who were chosen every year. If the required 6000 citizens didn't show up, special Pnyx Police would be sent out to round up more (just

imagine if that happened these days). These 6000 could accept or reject proposals as they wished.

The Law

I don't know about you, but I think the way the law was dished out in Ancient Greece leaves our system with a lot to be desired. There were no judges, lawyers or the rest of the pantomime we have to put up with in our courts today. All citizens were expected to *volunteer* for jury service (we *have* to attend) and would be properly paid for loss of earnings. The jury would be of 200 men instead of 12, which made it darned difficult to nobble them on their way to or from the court (or the loo). Crowds would turn up every day hoping to be chosen, as being a juror was thought to be a bit of a fab day out (*and* got you off work). Citizens had to speak for themselves, but could often use a flash speech writer to do the hard bit and make their case sound better. When the jury had heard all the different sides of the argument, they would all hand in little tokens ('guilty' or 'not guilty') which would then be counted up. This was brilliant because no one knew what the others had voted which greatly reduced the chance of being beaten up by angry rellies outside the court – simple but effective.

Ostracism (fancy word for 'exclusion')

This was totally brilliant. Each year a 'vote of ostracism' was held in the Assembly. Each citizen could scribble down the name of any politician that he didn't like on a piece of broken pottery (I'd need a sackful). If more than 6000 were cast for any one in particular, he'd have to leave the city for 10 years.

Oh boy, don't you wish we had that system for our present-day politicians? Trouble is, I doubt whether we'd have any of 'em left.

The Army

All able-bodied Athenian men of 20 or over were expected to fight if necessary, and, seeing as they had fresh wars practically every five minutes, it could be quite a full-time job. Older men of 50 and 60 were also called up but they weren't expected to go to the front line where the action was, unless they were losing (which I'd have thought was an even better excuse for staying behind*). Each of the ten Athenian tribes would be expected to rustle up a regiment and keep it fully stocked.

Soldier Types

Psilos

As in the rest of life, the better-off got the better jobs in the army. If you were really poor, you'd have to be a *psilo*. This was

*Coward! Ed

definitely not good, as you had no armour, no horse and, from the pictures I've seen, were only protected by a bit of old goat thrown over the shoulder and a rather silly-looking woolly hat. These psilos would be armed with stones (for the slinging of), clubs (for the swinging of) or, if very lucky, bows and arrows (for the shooting of).

Hoplites

Silly name I know, but these were the kind of Greek soldiers you see in all the pictures, wearing crested bronze helmets and full armour covering all the most vulnerable bits(!). Later they wore a *cuirass,* a kind of leather and bronze protective tunic. In front, they'd carry a round leather and bronze shield to protect most of their bodies, and for weapons they had an evil, razor-sharp, short sword and a long spear.

The Greek army invented the *phalanx* method of fighting which was rather neat and jolly effective. A wide block of soldiers (say twenty across and eight deep) with shields overlapping would march on the enemy. As each one in the front was injured (or worse) his place was taken by someone in the row behind, which meant that it looked as if the army was complete and always presented a solid wall of men. Enemy

generals, after a while, got used to this and thought it quite a laugh to attack the very vulnerable sides of the phalanx. I don't know about you, but I bet I'd be first in the rush to get to the middle of the back row.

Ekdromoi

Not to be recommended as a safe job with long-term prospects. In the fifth century the Greeks' Thracian enemies started using *peltasts*, tricky individuals who'd rush out from their lines and chuck spears right up, over and down into the middle of the Greek phalanxes. (Really! You could take someone's eye out doing things like that.) The *ekdromois'* job was to run out of the Greek phalanx (they were the fittest of the hoplites) and chase the naughty peltasts away.

It all sounds rather silly to me.

Cavalry

Probably the best job in the army, the cavalrymen used to charge about on their horses attacking the blocks or phalanxes of soldiers or just going out as scouts to look for someone to fight.

Useless Fact No. 537

The Spartans, in an attempt to beat the Athenians' allies, the Plataeans, built a huge wall round the Plataeans' city and sat around waiting for them to give in. When this eventually happened, the Spartans, in their inimitable way, killed all the men and took all their women as slaves. They then burned the city to the ground, saving all the roof timbers and doors. With these they built a huge pub (The Spartan Arms?), which sounds like a bit of a result to me.

The Navy

Greek military sailors couldn't rely on just the wind to get them along, so they had rows of oars down either side of their ships, sometimes up to three deep on different levels – the more the merrier. Some of the bigger, later ships had up to 180 men thrashing away – plus a load of archers at the front to do the actual fighting bit, which must have looked quite a sight. Although these boats were massive (up to 40 metres long), there was no room to sleep and not even a restaurant, toilet or bar (can you believe that?).

This, of course, meant that they couldn't go that far from the shore and had to tie up at night so the sailors could wade ashore, go to the lav and get some sleep. The fronts of their boats were made of bronze (all the better for ramming you with) and they always painted a massive eye (or two) on the front to frighten away the evil spirits – not to mention the enemy. The stripy sails would be taken down when battle commenced, presumably to stop them getting all those nasty arrow holes in 'em.

Useless Fact No. 539

When a ship was getting a bit past it, they'd strip it out and use it for transporting the horses.

Chapter 3

ART
AND ALL THAT
⊱≡ *CULTURAL STUFF*

Building Buildings

What's the first thing you need if you're going to spend a lot of
your time worshipping a load of made-up gods? Your head
examined?

No – jolly big and very impressive temples. The Greeks
were extremely good at this – so good that it is now reckoned
that all western European architecture that came along
afterwards (apart from maybe the pointy, archy Gothic style),
was derived (or nicked) from them. It's interesting to note
that the average individual wasn't nearly as bothered about
the homes *they* lived in, as long as their gods were nice and
comfy.

Style

Basically, once you'd peeled off all the decoration, Greek
buildings were dead simple: vertical columns holding up
horizontal lintels. These columns and lintels could be plain or
highly decorated, but it was the grace and dignity achieved by
the *spaces* in between them that made these vast stone things so
fab (not to mention that even after a couple of thousand years
many are still standing).

How to build a Greek Temple in Six Easy Stages

1. Ring a well-known architect and tell him what you want. We're lucky these days – in those ancient times there really weren't such things as proper, full-time architects (as far as we know). They tended to go in for master-builders, who more or less decided what the place was going to look like as they went along (sounds like Buckingham Palace!). This might not be as tricky as it seems (even when you look at something as colossal as the Parthenon in Athens) as this 'Greek style' simply evolved over hundreds of years. So it was a case of building something a bit like the last one, only different – well, sort of.

   Also, because there weren't masses of building regulations or nigglesome people like District Surveyors breathing down their necks ('you must have this many loos for this many people', or 'you can't put a door there', etc.*), when it came right down to it, they could do as they jolly well pleased.

2. To continue . . . In order to get things moving, see if you can win a war and take oodles of prisoners to rapidly convert into slaves. The Greeks were soon to find out that you can do practically anything if you've got enough human muscle.

3. Send some of your newly acquired slaves to your local quarry and ask them (very nicely) to bring you back lots of huge blocks of stone (and be quick about it).

4. Shape, or rather, get slaves to shape said stone into blocks (for walls) and round drum-like lumps (for columns).

*Calm down! Ed

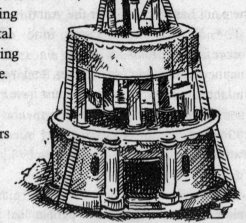

5. Using pulleys and levers, pile up drums, joining them with metal pegs to make columns; build walls joining blocks with metal cramps; and swing lintels into place. Piece of cake!

6. Send for stone-carvers, sculptors and frieze painters to tart whole place up.

. . . and Sculpture

Before the Golden Age, Greek sculpture and art had been a bit crude, heavily influenced (or copied) from the Egyptians (who never really got the hang of the human body). Stiff poses from front or side on, with identical faces and expressionless expressions.

Then in the Aeginetan period (580–480 BC), they began looking a little closer at the human body and the way it moved, hacking huge, curvy, anatomically correct figures out of rough stone (or using dollops of clay for little ones). They even made bronze statues but, sadly, most of these were melted down later by those uncouth Romans to make weapons and pots and pans.

Sculptures in Greek times were used to remember well-known people or even friends and relatives, a bit like we use photos today (only a tad more difficult to put in your wallet).

These days we tend to think that Greek sculptures were all in your actual natural stone colour but archaeologists now reckon they were, in fact, painted in bright, even garish colours (the paint has worn off over the years).

The Greeks also became fond of portraying their womenfolk without a stitch on (particularly beautiful imaginary babes like Aphrodite), and you'd be forgiven for thinking that all Greek women must have been 'perfect'. Not a bit of it, as you will realize if you go there now, they simply didn't bother immortalizing the ones they considered unattractive).

. . . and Music

Unlike the Romans, who thought music was a bit sissy, the Greeks were crazy about it, and used it at home and at religious festivals. Plato (their top philosopher/poet) once claimed that music was for the soul and gymnastics was for the body, which is pretty blinking obvious when you come to think of it.

Unfortunately we haven't a clue what their stuff sounded like. It's all very well seeing paintings of their instruments but unfortunately you can't hear pictures* and unfortunately (we presume) they forgot to write down the tunes. I bet, however, that Greek music then wasn't like the dreadful (in my opinion) plinky-plonky stuff you hear in their restaurants now.

Useless Fact No. 541
The lyre, one of the Greeks' top instruments, was a cross between a harp and a guitar. It was apparently invented by a god called Hermes who, when little, found a turtle feeding on the grass. He

*You surprise me. Ed

promptly choked the poor thing (nice kid) and scooped its insides out (I wonder what Rolf Harris would have to say about that). He then inserted various lengths of reed-stalk into the shell, stretched ox-hide round it and inserted the wooden 'horns' of the lyre. Then he stretched seven strings made of sheep gut (crikey, talk about Animal Hospital, this is Animal Graveyard). To this day turtles, oxen and sheep (and me) run a mile when they hear the lyre.

Useless Fact No. 547

Pythagoras, the brainiac who discovered how to measure triangles, also discovered that by pressing hard on certain strings at certain points, notes and even octaves can be changed.

Useless Fact No. 549*

The pan pipes, the instrument which I hate more than any other in the whole world and which seem to be on the soundtrack of every programme about South America, were allegedly invented by a young god called Pan who was half-man/half-goat (typical half-goat behaviour). His best friend was called ECHO . . . ECHO . . . ECHO . . . ECHO . . . ECHO

*That's enough Useless Facts now. Ed

Useless Fact No. 550

Another really interesting fact about the musical tastes of the Ancient Greeks is that —*

. . . and Poetry

The Greeks were poetry mad, and guys like Homer were treated like gods. He wrote this huge, seemingly never-ending poem about all the Greek heroes, which had been passed down through the generations, but which had been carelessly lost during the Dark Ages. Many Greeks would be expected to recite his *Iliad* and *Odyssey* from memory. The reciters were called *rhapsodes,* and they did it for a living at festivals or even at smart little private dos.

. . . and Drama

At one point a poet decided to invite a couple of mates to help out with the reading, and before they knew it they had the first *play* on their hands. Greek plays weren't like the ones we have now, however, as they didn't have any scenery, no real action (car chases, etc.), no roof (they were always outside), no women (they were always inside – cooking) and – if tragedies – no jokes.

. . . and Fables

If they couldn't face the endless poems about gods and heroes, the Greeks went in for fables, which were little stories with a message, written by chaps like Aesop. Aesop was an ex-slave who was like a travelling pedlar, trading

*I said, that's enough! Ed

stories as opposed to pots and pans (or women's underwear). Stories with morals like 'Don't count your chickens before they're hatched' (Aesop), 'Slow and steady wins the race' (Aesop) or 'Never jump off a moving bus' (me).

I CAN'T COUNT ANYWAY

Useless Fact No. 551

Unfortunately, Aesop took one of his own morals ('The gods help those who help themselves') rather too much to heart. Having become extremely popular at the court of King Croesus, he was given a huge sum of money to distribute to the good citizens of Delphi. When he decided to hang on to the loot, the Delphians, understandably, got a bit narked and chucked him off a high cliff.

Fat lot of good the gods did Aesop.

Chapter 4

KEEPING COOL IN ANCIENT GREECE

We know quite a bit about what the Ancient Greeks looked like through examining all the thousands of carvings they left on their statues and gravestones. We know, for example, that the big look for the better-off women was 'the simpler and paler the better'. Anything approaching a suntan was seen as desperately common, probably because the lowly peasant women, who worked in the sun all day, were usually as brown as well-done pitta bread.

Most women wore a *chiton* – one piece of cloth about two metres by four metres, which was woven at home and draped over the body in different and often complicated ways, secured by a belt or girdle at the waist or with a brooch at the shoulder. When going out, especially if it was a bit chilly, they would throw a *himation* or cloak over the shoulders. Men's dress was much the same.

YOU LOOK LOVELY

THANK YOU DARLING

But everyone knows roughly what the Greeks looked like, so let's push on.

Useless Fact No. 552
Greek women were some of the first to wear high heels on their shoes to make them look taller, but usually they went barefoot or wore sandals.

Pale and Interesting

It's odd to think that we now go to Greece to bronze our bodies, for if an Ancient Greek lady (or should I say a lady that lived in Ancient Greece) noticed she was getting a slight tan from going out in the hot sun, she'd plaster her face with white lead to look paler (or use a hot slave with a shade to keep her cool). As our good Queen Elizabeth (the first) could have told her (had she not come along centuries later), it wasn't that smart a move, as the lead had a nasty habit of eating into people's faces and leaving them with rather horrid scars.

Anyway, fashionably pale Miss Greece would slap a little red berry juice on her cheeks to put back some of the colour she'd just taken away, and then smother herself in overpowering scent. Oh well – takes all sorts, I suppose.

Chapter 5

FARMING – AND EATING
 THE RESULTS

If you were Greek and you weren't living in the city being an artist, philosopher, poet or something clever like that, you'd more than likely be a farmer. Actually, a lot of those brainy folk in the towns had farms as well, to provide them with an income (poetry, philosophy and writing never did pay that well*). But they didn't want to get their own personal hands dirty, so they would have their land farmed by a servant, his family and a couple of tame slaves. Slaves were mostly prisoners of internal Greek wars and were thus Greek. (And they didn't have nearly as a bad a time of it as they'd've had if they'd been foreign.) Farms in Ancient Greece weren't that different from the ones you get these days (in Greece). A couple of dusty, rocky acres surrounding a dusty, rocky farmhouse.

Home on the Farm

Most of the land could only sustain a few scruffy goats, mooching about on a baking hot, stony hillside, a handful of stunted olive trees for shade, and, if you were lucky, a grape vine in the back yard. Greek smallholders would also try to grow a few peas or beans for their own use.

They'd generally keep a bee or two (well, a couple of

*You should know. Ed

thousand actually) for honey, which was used to sweeten their everyday tipple: goat's milk. The few crops that there were (most of the wheat had to be imported) were grown on the flat coastal plains and the handful of inland areas that weren't continually gasping for the old H_2O.

Olives were essential to Greek life. They used the oil instead of butter (much healthier), for illuminating their houses, for cooking, for mixing in beauty products, and of course, there were always the olive stones for flicking at each other after supper.

Useless Fact No. 555

The olive tree was so important to the Greek way of life that anyone caught cutting one down or pulling one up was deemed to be breaking the law. It was considered an act of high tree-son.

Poor Grub

It seems that throughout the ancient world most poor people ate the same things – porridge and rough gritty bread (made with barley). The Greeks also managed to find a variable supply of figs, onions, carrots, that funny white cheese called feta which you get in all good Greek restaurants and, of course, goats . . . everywhere you looked – goats. The goat would supply them voluntarily with milk, on a good day, and *involuntarily* with meat (for eating), skin (for wearing) and hair (for weaving), on a bad one. If they were lucky the Greeks would catch the odd hare or deer or wild pig, but if they were unlucky, the odd snake would catch them while out hunting. People who lived near the sea lived almost exclusively on fish, squid (*calamari* in Greek) and octopus (*taco* in Japanese*) – as they still do.

Richer is Better

Rich people ate much the same stuff as the poor, but there'd be more of it and a better choice. Surprise, surprise. The biggest difference was that there'd be gaggles of hand slave-maidens (is that right?) to dish it out. Both rich and poor would drink gallons of wine, usually mixed with water, and served from big Greek urns. Please don't ask me what a big Greek urns.**

*Are you going mad? Ed
**Well done! You've managed to include the worst joke in the world. Ed
I aim to please. JF

Chapter 6

FUN AND GAMES IN ANCIENT GREECE

Fun First

The Greeks loved giving parties. Well, to be fair, only half of the Greeks loved parties. Women weren't invited. Maybe I should rephrase that . . . *Wives* and *daughters* weren't invited. Boys could sometimes sit on the sidelines and watch what went on – as part of their education.

How to Run a Greek Party

- Be male.
- Invite all your male friends – and any unattached females who might be short of something to do that night.
- When your guests arrive, have your slaves take them into the *andron* (party room).
- Get the slaves to wash their feet and hands (the guests' feet and hands, that is).
- Then have your slaves serve them several courses of lavish food and as much wine as they can drink out of a huge jug called a *krater*.
- Call in the jesters, musicians and dancing babes.
- Depending on how riotous the proceedings are becoming: sit around discussing the world, universe, or the meaning of life (or Gary Lineker); gamble with dice; or play drunken games like *Kottabos*.

Useless Fact No. 556

Kottabos was definitely the silliest game you've ever heard of. Each guest waits till he's got a small amount of wine in his cup, while, in the centre of the room, a slave sets up a vertical post with a little bronze disc balanced on the top. The object of the game was to hurl the contents of your cup across the room with the intention of knocking off the disc. Pretty intellectual, eh! Sounds like the sort of thing you see in trendy wine bars these days.

. . . and Games

Again, mostly for men (women weren't really allowed to have fun – or games). Athletics was all the rage with the Ancient

Greeks and I suppose its main purpose was to keep the lads in tip-top condition for when they had to play at soldiers. As well as the hundreds of little local gatherings, there were the big ones: the Isthmian, Nemean, Pythian and, of course, the Olympic Games. These were a magnet for every relatively fit male in Greece.

The Olympics
The Olympic Games started in 776 BC and took place in Olympia (where else?) in honour of top god Zeus. They were held every five days and lasted four years*.

Married women, true to form, weren't even allowed in the audience (or anywhere near Olympia come to that) during the competition.

Useless Fact No. 557
Although women weren't allowed to compete in the Olympics, they did have a little Games of their own called *Heraia*, but there were only three races and, unlike the men, they kept all their kit on while running. Men, by the way, always competed in the nude, which might have been why the ladies weren't allowed. Shame – they might have found it quite a laugh (if you know what I mean).

Games not War
One brilliant aspect of their passion for athletics was that the Greeks stopped fighting all their little individual wars, just so that they could go to the Games – but they started them again the minute they were over. Every four years messengers would travel throughout Greece wearing special olive wreaths (and probably not much else) to pronounce a Truce of Sport.

* I think you might have that the wrong way round. Ed
Just seeing if you're paying attention. JF

Unlike today when a host city for the Games has to fork out millions for new stadia, and all the paraphernalia that goes with them, Olympia had magnificent specially built buildings, including a stadium for 40,000 people. The visitors usually camped on the vast plains outside the city.

There were five events in the Ancient Olympics: running, wrestling, jumping, discus and javelin throwing. There was none of that ludicrous synchronized swimming or loony ski dancing (to name but two of many) that we have to endure these days. Being strictly amateurs (whatever that means), their reward was just a poxy old olive wreath.

The most famous event was the *pentathlon* involving all five events, in which every athlete competed to find the best all-rounder.

Useless Fact No. 559

I have it on good authority (well, my mate Kev) that the current Olympic committee are thinking of including ballroom dancing and even darts next time round.

The poor old Greeks would turn in their Grecian graves (just imagine nude darts!).

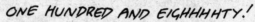

ONE HUNDRED AND EIGHHHHTY!

OLIVE-LEAF

Useless Fact No. 562

The Greeks never got the hang of running round a circuit (so they weren't *that* bright) and simply ran up and down, turning round at each end. Come to think of it, running round in circles like we do today is probably just as silly.

Useless Fact No. 566*

Long-jumpers carried weights in both hands – about a kilogram each – which they swung forward as they took off. Apparently, it made them go further. They hadn't invented high-jumping yet. Shame really, as they could have carried gas balloons or attached springs on their shoes (had they worn any).

*Any chance of a useful fact one of these days? Ed

Other Events

At the smaller sporting meetings there were many other events and quite good prizes were dished out for the winners. For example:

Boxing

Two men would fight, totally naked, except for leather thongs wrapped round their . . . knuckles, until one or other was beaten unconscious or gave in. They could punch or slap each other any way they liked. The prizes were as follows:

- The winner would receive a mule.
- The loser would receive a two-handed cup (to keep his newly displaced teeth in, perhaps).

Chariot Racing

As many as 40 chariots would tear round two posts set in the ground, having been released from a special gate. The inevitable accidents were the most fun of all. The prizes were rather fab, as well.

- First prize was a woman who was good at cooking and handiwork.
- Second prize was a horse (I'm relieved they were in that order).
- Third was a nice new bronze cauldron.
- Fourth, two *talents* of gold.

Wrestling

The winner of an 'upright' wrestling match had to throw his opponent down three times; in a 'ground' match he had to fight till the other guy gave in; but in the *Pankration* he could do anything except for biting or gouging his opponent's eyes out. The prizes this time might cause my lady readers some distress:

- The winner got a large tripod for hanging pots over the fire.

- The sad loser got a 'good-looking woman'.

Chapter 7

WOMEN AND GIRLS IN ANCIENT GREECE

I think it was Aristotle (the famous Greek philosopher) who said that women were just unfinished men and simply a receptacle to grow babies in. Anyone got anything to say about that? The poor girls in Ancient Greece started out being dominated by their fathers and brothers, then by their husbands and then, would you believe, by their sons. How general this was is difficult to say, but we do know that women led a very sheltered life and were not allowed any say in how things were run. They weren't allowed to own property or have any dealings with lawyers. A woman's function was to look after her old man and do all the household jobs including weaving and making the clothes. The poorer they were the worse it was (so what's new?).

Out and About

A woman seldom went out, and if she did, it was usually to some religious festival or (if very lucky) to visit a friend. Even so, she had to be accompanied by a slave. The reason for this is obvious. Because the men were so feckless and unfaithful, they didn't want their own women falling pray to people like themselves. Sounds fair . . . Men, on the other hand, were allowed to have mistresses and throw parties where they could invite their male friends and even prostitutes. Homosexuality was also all the rage and nobody batted an eye if young Jimmius didn't seem to like the girls much. In fact, both Plato and Socrates, their finest philosophers, were well-known for being gay.

Divorce

If a woman's husband became fed up with her (or fancied a newer model) he simply told her of his intention in front of witnesses: job done. It was virtually impossible for a woman to do the same, however badly she was treated.

Whose Fault?

A lot of the blame for men's attitude to women could be laid at the feet of the gods. The male gods were always leaping in and out of bed with mortal women (and each other, by all accounts). Mind you, as all the stories of what the gods were like were made up by men in the first place, this wasn't really fair. A Greek woman who became pregnant outside of marriage quite often claimed *it was the gods what done it*.

HONEST DAD - HE _SAID_ HE WAS A GOD

Any lady gods that went with mortal men weren't into one-night stands like their male counterparts, and tended to settle down into long relationships.

Nearly Rude Bit

The Ancient Greeks, it must be said, were absolutely sex-mad and went in for lots of very rude pictures and even ruder poetry, which my editor won't let me tell you about.*

*I'm sure they don't want to know. Ed
I'm sure they do! JF

Chapter 8

GREEK SCIENCE

It's all right for us . . . when we go out in a boat, we're pretty sure that as soon as we get out of sight of land we're *not* going to fall off the edge of the earth. And we know that the sun *isn't* just a little hot yellow ball that mysteriously comes up in the east and disappears in the west. The ancient Greeks, however, knew none of this, so you can imagine what they were up against when trying to make some sense of the world they lived in.

But they didn't want to know how everything worked just so they could harness it and make it their slave or make themselves money as we do now. They were simply ravenous for knowledge for its own sake (which is much easier when you don't know much in the first place). It's important to realize that this was the first time scientists or 'natural philosophers' (as they were known then) had made any attempt to move away from all that old myth and magic that had held primitive man and his primitive wife back for so long.

Bonkers Greek Theories

To begin with, though, the poor devils stumbled around in the dark, coming up with some wild and wacky ideas in an attempt to find what *it* was all about. Try these for size.

Thales of Miletus thought that everything, including me and presumably you, came from water. What a drip!

🐌 *Anaximander,* who thought Thales' theory a bit wet, preferred to believe that the universe came from a huge pulsating mass called 'the boundless' which turned out to be slime. Boundless slime? No thank you.

🐌 *Anaximenes,* his student, believed that because we all breathed air, this air must have turned into clouds, water, earth, stone, flesh, bones and even life insurance salesmen. He also claimed that we lived on a sort of 'desert island disc' floating around in space. Hey man – groovy!

🐌 *Heraclitus* would have none of this and claimed we were all born out of fire, on the basis that because everything in the universe is constantly changing, and fire is constantly changing too, they must be all part and parcel of the same thing. Back to the rather singed drawing board for you, Heraclitus.

Nearly Right

There were thousands of these ideas but in amongst them all one guy very nearly scored a bullseye. A loony called Democritus suddenly came up with this madcap theory that the whole universe was made up of millions of tiny, indivisible things (atoms) whizzing about in space and suddenly joining together with the aid of weeny little hooks (velcro?) to form anything from wombats to pop-up toasters*. This idea was picked up again in the seventeenth century by a French Jesuit called Gassendi and later by John Dalton to form the basis for modern atomic theory. Cripes!

Useless Fact No. 569

Democritus had a problem. He lusted after every woman he clapped eyes on, and could hardly control himself. Being the brilliant scientist that he no doubt was, he came up with a scintillating solution. He blinded himself. Job done!

Prometheus

The Greeks looked to the myth of Prometheus as inspiration for their scientific enquiry. Prometheus apparently took fire from the boss god Zeus and gave it to us lot (mankind). Once we had fire we could cook, smelt iron, fire pots, light fags (whoops) and generally progress scientifically. Fat lot of good it did Prometheus, however – Zeus punished him for helping us humans and neglecting the gods. Read on.

Useless Myth No. 571

Prometheus' punishment was rather unpleasant. Zeus had the poor bloke chained to a mountain and made his rather evil eagles peck away at his liver every day (luckily it was renewed every night). How offal!

* Sorry, this is all a bit too technical for me – I don't think. Ed

Who, Why and When?

But the philosophers were into much bigger ponders, like how the heavens moved (and who moved 'em), whether the earth was going to blow up sooner or later (remember, they get quite a few earthquakes and volcanoes down that way), and whether or not there was any order or sense to this thing they called the world. Here are a few of the big names in early learning and their attempts at explaining the whole sorry business.

Hippocrates, 460–377 BC

Always labelled 'the father of medicine', he snatched the whole health issue away from religion and magic. Up till then, all the best diseases like epilepsy and leprosy were believed to have been delivered by some grumpy god or other. Hippocrates was much more interested in the environment in which the disease had been nurtured in the first place. The dirtier, the better, I presume.

Aristotle, 384–322 BC

Aristotle is generally regarded as the Big Daddy of science, though supporters of Gallileo (much later) try to give *him* the credit (actually, who cares?). Aristotle was about as clever a chap as you could find, studying every avenue of science with equal passion, and, much more to the point, in a proper, methodical way (for a change). He was still a fan of old Socrates' original recipe that went like this (sort of):

> Realize how important you are and don't take anything for granted. Get to the truth by asking your own questions and don't believe anything anyone else tells you.

That's what I always say.

Know Your Place

Aristotle believed that everything in nature has its place. Why do fish swim in water? Why do stones fall to earth? Why are some men born rich and others poor? Why does Elton John's hair never seem to grow any longer? Because, he claimed, it's their nature. Aristotle had a few great students, one of whom went on to be Alexander the Great. I suppose you can't get much greater than that.

Archimedes, 287–212 BC

People like Archimedes (and me) make most others look plain

stupid. He was a mathematician living in Syracuse, Sicily, and was a mate of King Hieron II. One day Hieron asked him if he could think of a way of finding out whether his crown was pure gold or not (he thought his personal crownologist was diddling him). Archimedes pondered on the prob for weeks but to no avail. It was only when he finally decided to take a bath (some sweaty Greek, eh!) that it came to him. For every bit of his body (yes, even that bit) that went into the water, an equal amount went over the side (the bath had been full up right to the top.)

Out into the street he ran, stark naked, waving (everything) at the passers-by. 'Eureka!' ('I've discovered it') he yelled (and so did they, I should imagine*). Back indoors he put the crown in the bath and measured the water it displaced. He then weighed the crown and put an equal amount of pure gold in the bath. It should have displaced the same amount of water as the crown . . . Unfortunately for the crown-maker (who'd been

NOT INVENTED YET

NOW, WHERE DID I DISPLACE THAT SOAP?

*Stop it! Ed

mixing gold with cheaper, lighter metals) it displaced *more* water than it should've, and very soon he was left somewhat short of the necessary equipment (headwise) to even try a crown on.

Archimedes went on to discover levers, war machines, catapults and the still-used 'Archimedes Screw' (a gizmo for lifting water from one level to another).

Useless Fact No. 573

When the Romans captured Syracuse in 212 BC, Archimedes was indoors doing his sums. A Roman soldier burst into his room and Archimedes, somewhat niggled, yelled, 'Man, do not disturb me.' Unfortunately, the soldier wasn't particularly into mathematical calculations and promptly cut him to ribbons. That's Romans for you.

Great Greek Discoveries

Here are a few more things the Greeks discovered:

- 28th May, 585 BC was the first specific date ever recorded in history. There was an eclipse of the sun – and probably someone's birthday.

- Eratosthenes (try saying that while chewing a toffee) measured the earth's circumference and wasn't that far out. His tape measure said 24,662 miles (it's really 24,822). Not much difference, but I suppose you might mind if you lived on the bit he left out.

- Aristotle put 500 animals into eight classes (sounds like my old school).

Alcmaeon of Croton was the first person to dissect another person (and get away with it). He did it for the highest of medical motives.

Empodocles came up with this bizarre theory that the heart is the centre of the blood system. He was an odd bod, so they say. One day, when fed up with not

SURGERY

Taking Work Home!

being made into a god (I know the feeling), he leapt into the fiery mouth of Mount Etna, the volcano, to prove he was immortal. Unfortunately it seems he wasn't and was never seen again.*

The optical telegraph was invented. Sounds pretty flash, eh? Don't get too excited – it was just a series of bonfires used to signal from one hilltop to another and so on and so on. Who couldn't have thought of that? Everyone, apparently.

Anacharsis, a sailor, fed up with never knowing where he or his boat were in the morning, invented the anchor.

Geometry

There was this chap called Euclid who organized all the Greeks' random mathematical thinking in a whizzy little book called *Elements*. It doesn't seem possible but people were still

*Let that be a lesson to you. Ed

being taught from this book as late as the 1920s. As you all must know, Euclid supplied the first model of an axiomatic deductive system* and his work was taken up by Newton, Galilleo, and Halley (of comet fame).

Astronomy

It didn't take long for the Greeks to realize that the world was round (we could've told 'em that) and in 275 BC Aristarchus of Samos suggested that the sun was in the centre of our solar system. Most people thought this a real joke, so when, some time later (in the second century AD), a famous stargazer called Ptolomy (pronounced 'tolomy') worked out a geocentric model of the cosmos with us, the earth, at the centre, everyone clapped.

Shame he was wrong! Fortunately for him (but not for the rest of mankind) he explained the whole business so convincingly that it took centuries to overthrow it. It was that famous duo Galileo and Kepler in the seventeenth century who finally proved that Scunthorpe is the centre of the solar system.**

All Over

Boringly, when the Emperor Justinian closed the Academy and Lyceum in Athens and the Arabs destroyed the library in Alexandria, all scientific activity ground to a halt in Europe. There wasn't to be a twinkle of light until the mid-fifteenth century when the Turks nicked a load of Greek manuscripts from Constantinople and brought them back to Europe.

*A what? Ed
**Behave! It's the sun. Ed

Chapter 9

GODS-U-LIKE

It was always claimed in the Bible that God (our God, that is) wanted Man to be made in His image . . . but not *quite* as well, which, though a little conceited, seems fair enough if you're God. The Greeks, though wanting their gods (note the little 'g') to be just like them looks-wise, required them to be stronger, braver, cleverer and altogether much better(er). Otherwise there'd have been no point summoning them whenever they were in a spot of bother.

Here are a few of the probs you might come across as an ancient Greek along with some of the relevant gods you might call upon:

Problem 1:
You are out fishing in your boat on a jolly nice day. Suddenly a huge storm blows up and threatens to throw you in the drink. Who do you call?

Answer:

POSEIDON, and pretty darn quick. He was the god of the deep and the sign on his office door said *Ruler of the Seas*. He lived, as you might have guessed, underwater, and that was where he kept his somewhat damp white horses and somewhat tarnished gold chariot. When feeling a little grumpy he'd whip up a storm or hurricane, just to cheer himself up. If asked nicely, he could also reverse the procedure.

Problem 2:

A terrible hurricane breaks out on land threatening to destroy your property. Who should you contact?

Answer:

Apart from the insurance company, go right to the top and try ZEUS (Poseidon's older brother). He was the boss of all the other gods and godlets. His main job was to rule the heavens and he did this often disguised as a bull, a shower of gold or a swan. Each to his own.

MY ROOF'S JUST COME DOWN IN ONE OF YOUR STORMS!

ZEUS

Problem 3:

You've got this girlfriend, see, and she's a right grump – never smiling and always giving you a hard time. What do you do?

Answer:

Call on APHRODITE, goddess of love and beauty. She could usually get anyone (girl or boy) 'in the right mood' (nudge, nudge!). Aphrodite, herself a real babe by all accounts (Greek accounts, that is), was born at sea and came to shore in a scallop shell (cramped and smelly or what?). It says in my encyclopedia that she always wore a golden belt, which apparently made her irresistible (which is not surprising if it was all she wore). If you were a *woman* and had an unfaithful boyfriend or husband (and if Aphrodite couldn't do the trick) you could try HERA, Zeus's wife, who was the protector of women and marriage.

Problem 4:

Your mates have got this band and they want you to join. The only problem is that you're tone deaf, can't play as much as a comb and paper and can't think of any songs. Who can help?

Answer:

Try APOLLO. He doubled as god of music and of poetry. Busy lad, Apollo: his other responsibilities involved looking after science and healing and . . . oh yes, truth.

Problem 5:

You've got this rubber plant that's looking a little poorly. As there's no *Gardeners' Question Time* on the radio, who do you write to?

Answer:

DEMETER, the Goddess of all Plants. Demeter, it must be said, once had a spot of bother herself. Not with plants, but with her daughter . . . who was kidnapped. When Demeter went off to search for her, it brought about winter for the first time. When she got her back, winter turned into spring and then summer. How simply charming.

Problem 6:

You're not feeling too well, and think you might be about to pop your clogs. What's next?

Answer:

Better start making your peace with HADES (also known as PLUTO, and brother of Poseidon and Zeus) as he was the Greek god of the dead, and ruled the underworld (also known as Hades). I suppose a job's a job.

Sacrifice

There were gods for all occasions and not one single Greek ever doubted their power. The only payment the gods insisted on was regular sacrifice (of a sheep, ox or goatular nature). Unlike the Christians (coming soon*), the Greeks had no concept of sin, so had absolutely no worries about what would happen to their souls in the afterlife.

SORRY, BUT I THINK THIS MIGHT HURT YOU MORE THAN IT HURTS ME.

* If you call five centuries 'soon'. Ed

Oracled Out

If a Greek person couldn't manage to speak to a god directly, he'd go to a priest or priestess, called an *oracle*, who'd do it for him. The place they did it in was also called an *oracle* and the actual words the gods spoke were called *oracles* as well (bit confusing, eh!).

There were quite a few *oracles* dotted around the country and thousands would attend. These chats with the gods were so important that hardly a new war, a new law, a new government or a new dinner party was planned without their say-so.

Biggest and Best

The most important *oracle,* run by a high priestess called Pythia in Delphi, became so popular that her yearly sessions had to become weekly.

They went like this.

 Pythia would go into her little room and leap into a tub of holy water, drink from a sacred spring, and then inhale burning leaves (and we can all guess what *those* were*).

 The priests would then come in bowing, scraping and generally grovelling and proceed to ask the questions that they'd been asked to ask by the punters outside.

 Pythia would then mumble something pretty obscure and the priest's job was to interpret what she said (money for old rope if you ask me).

Useless Fact No. 577

At the Corinth oracle the visitor was requested to speak to the high altar, upon which the gods would reply. When archaeologists were rooting around the base of the altar they found a tunnel large

*Can we? Ed

enough to take a priest and a funnel leading to a hole just where the customer would be standing. Could it be that it wasn't the god's voice that he heard? Surely not.

COULD YOU SPEAK UP A BIT

Mirror, Mirror on the Wall

If you wanted to know things of a little more mundane or personal nature – like whether to marry a particular girl or boy (presumably you'd know which), or buy a new sports chariot, you'd ring the soothsayer or fortune-teller who was supposed to be good at looking into the future. These people, I imagine, were like the terrible, whiskery old frauds that waylay you at fairgrounds (crystal balls, tea leaves, palm-reading and all the rest of the mumbo-jumbo).

Useless Fact No. 580

One such lady soothsayer, Cassandra, who lived in Troy, warned the powers that be not to accept any strange gifts – especially wooden horses. They didn't listen and when, by sheer chance, a rather large one turned up (as they do) outside the city gates, in the middle of a siege, they brought it in without a moment's thought – only to find it full of nasty, and extremely cross, enemy soldiers.

This is said to be the origin of the saying 'Never trust a Greek bearing gifts.'

Cults and Such

You know all those bizarre and loony religious sects that seem to delight in killing all their members (usually in the USA) – well, they probably developed from the Greek cults. Thousands of people, not content with worshipping the straightforward, ordinary public gods, joined together to carry out highly secret and weird ceremonies.*

Most popular were two lady gods, Zeus's wife Hera and her daughter, Persephone who got laid – sorry – waylaid by god Hades.

*How do you know they were weird if they were secret? Ed

ᗞ TIME'S UP

Sorry, but that's your lot. Sadly (or not!), I've used up all my words. I do hope you know a little more about the Greeks than you did. If you knew it all anyway, then might I suggest *you* write the next book and I'll take a few days off. Anyway, you can't really complain – what else can you buy for £1.99 that would bring such pleasure and intellectual stimulation?*

Seriously (me, serious?), if you really are fascinated by the Greeks, your local library will have tons on the subject, but if, like me, you feel you know just about enough and want to know what happened next, why don't you blow another couple of quid and buy my book on the Romans? I should have finished it by then.

*Might I suggest a few copies of the *Beano*? Ed

JOHN FARMAN
HISTORY IN A HURRY
Very good, very short, very funny (and very cheap).

Aztecs	0 330 35247 4	£1.99
Ancient Egypt	0 330 35248 2	£1.99
Ancient Greece	0 330 35249 0	£1.99
Romans	0 330 35250 4	£1.99
Tudors	0 330 35251 2	£1.99
Middle Ages	0 330 35252 0	£1.99
Victorians	0 330 35253 9	£1.99
Vikings	0 330 35254 7	£1.99
Dark Ages	0 330 37086 3	£1.99
Ancient China	0 330 37087 1	£1.99
Stuarts	0 330 37088 X	£1.99
French Revolution	0 330 37089 8	£1.99